13 & COUNTiNG:
Be the *Difference!*

○○○○○○○ Engaging Bullying-Prevention Activities
That Promote Social Skills and Executive Function

by

TAMARA ZENTIC, M.S.

BOYS TOWN
Press®

Boys Town, Nebraska

13 & Counting: Be the Difference!
Copyright © 2014 by Father Flanagan's Boys' Home

ISBN 978-1-934490-59-4

Published by Boys Town Press
14100 Crawford St.
Boys Town, Nebraska 68010

Printed in the United States
10 9 8 7 6 5 4 3 2 1

**For a Boys Town Press catalog, call 1-800-282-6657
or visit our website: BoysTownPress.org**

 Boys Town Press is the publishing division of Boys Town, a national organization serving children and families.

Table of Contents

Introduction

Kickball was the most popular recess game at Alcott Elementary. The captains would get to choose the teams. Of course, those who were really good, or at least not bad, would get selected first. Their faces would beam with pride while all the rest of us would stand and wait to be picked. The biggest fear was to be chosen last. You would just hope and pray that you would at least be second to last, because that was SOOO much better than being last. It was downright humiliating to be picked dead last!

Well, sometime around my third- or fourth-grade year, I realized – well let's put it this way – I KNEW I was never going to be picked first, second, sixth, or even ninth, unless it was my birthday and I got to be captain for the day! I did not inherit the highly sought-after kickball genes. I was more of a kickball klutz!

Fortunately for me, I had a couple of friends who felt the same way I did. So because there was safety and peace in numbers, we decided to play on the playground equipment and jump rope during our recess time. Life was good... until that day in the lunch line. I remember it vividly, even after all these years, because it was "Chili Day." "Chili Day" was infamous. The "Chili Day" of my era was not like the "Chili Day" of the 21st century. "Chili Day," for us, was sacred! You did not want to be sick on "Chili Day." The chili was homemade and contained just the right balance of meat and beans, and the sauce was seasoned with a savory, perfect concoction of chili seasonings. You got an entire bowl full and it was far superior to anyone's lunch from home. You DID NOT trade food on "Chili Day."

As good as the chili was, though, it was second to the main event on the tray – a warm, mouthwatering, appetite-provoking, freshly baked cinnamon roll. I can still visualize the way it would wrap around itself, culminating in a frosting-covered pinnacle.

They were out-of-this-world delicious! You guarded your roll with your life!

The smell of chili and freshly baked cinnamon rolls would linger in our school hallways for hours. You didn't mind standing in line for lunch on those days, because you could just visualize and anticipate the meal that was waiting for you around the corner. Well, that is exactly where I was at that particular moment – standing in line for a "Chili Day" lunch, when it happened….

Maurice was new to our school. He gained friends quickly and easily because he was athletic, fast, funny, and most of us were afraid of him. He always acted nice to the teachers, but when the teachers weren't looking, he would say something mean or act like he was going to punch you. Maurice made me nervous. I made an effort to stay off his radar. I usually accomplished this rather well… until that "Chili Day." I was halfway back in line when Maurice arrived from lunch recess. He came to the lunch line and walked right up to me, looked me squarely in the face, pointed to his eye, and said, "Look what YOU made me do! YOU made me get hit in the eye with the kickball and now I have a black eye! This is YOUR fault and I'll be waiting for you after school! I'm going to BEAT YOU UP, so you better be ready!" He then cut in line in front of me and just glared at me. Suddenly, I wasn't hungry anymore. I had a lump the size of Texas in my stomach. Not even chili and a cinnamon roll could make it go away.

I went through the rest of the line in a daze. Somehow I made it through lunch, but I hardly touched my chili and ended up giving half my cinnamon roll away. My friends did what all good friends do; they rallied around me and watched Maurice's

every move. They strategized and fretted with me, but when it came right down to it, none of them could walk home after school with me that day.

I was the "Lone Ranger." I thought about going to the nurse and acting like I was sick so my mom would come and get me early. But I knew it would be inconvenient for her to come and pick me up. The afternoon wore on. My mind was engaged on one thought and one thought only: "Run For Your Life!" So, at 3:20, that is exactly what I did. I bolted out the front door and ran as fast as I could. I ran and ran and ran. I lived 13 blocks from school, but that day it might as well have been 130 blocks. I ran all the way home, strategically running down streets that weren't even on my normal route home. I must have checked over my shoulder at least a dozen times to see if he was behind me. I was exhausted when I ran in the front door, but I had made it. I had survived! At that moment I was safe, and maybe, just maybe, by tomorrow, he would forget.

Maurice's eye was even more bruised the next day. He glared at me and waved his fist at me when the teacher wasn't looking. I could hardly keep from crying. I could feel the lump in my throat and the one in my stomach getting tighter and tighter. Midway through the afternoon, my teacher handed me a note from the office. The note said that my mom would be picking me up after school that day. I had a scheduled ride home. I felt as lucky as a kid in a candy store. I was saved! I wouldn't have to face Maurice that day!

When I returned to school the next day, Maurice still glared at me and raised his fist. I had my friends talk to him, but he didn't seem to want to change his mind. My stomach kept twisting and turning day after day. I would avoid him and strategically flee after school each day. This went on for weeks. Maurice never did beat me up physically, but I was beat, from the start, emotionally. I lived in a constant state of fear. I wished Maurice had never existed.

You always knew where you stood with Monica. That girl did not have a filter on her mouth. I don't think she even knew what a filter was. She would say anything that came to mind and wouldn't feel bad in the least. She was sassy and defiant, and would poke fun of someone right to their face. She would laugh loudly and even point her finger at them while the other person turned twenty shades of red out of embarrassment. Even with the teachers Monica did not hold back. If you had just walked in from outside on a windy day, she would point and laugh and shriek, "You look like a witch!" She was a challenge on a constant basis.

Monica was a bully. She constantly teetered on the brink between being in trouble and staying out of trouble. At times, she knew how far she could take her aggression toward others without getting caught. Yet, at other times, she unleashed her venom without fear of punishment. Such was the case between Monica and Steven.

Steven was your average boy. He got fairly good grades in every subject. He was a little ornery at times, but not bad in any sense of the word. He got along with most of the students, and most of the time, he didn't get into trouble at school. Unfortunately for

Steven, Monica had decided she didn't really like him. Steven had excluded her during a PE activity and Monica was known to hold a grudge.

On this particular day, she had reminded Steven that he was, in her words, a "loser"! Monica had told him that all of her friends were now mad at him for leaving her out. Steven told her that he could choose whomever he wanted to in PE. Monica did not like that, so she decked him. She punched him right across the face and called him a "loser" again. At this point, a teacher intervened and took them both to the office. Monica was asked why she had hit Steven, and she answered that it was because he had excluded her. She went on to say that when she confronted Steven about it, he told her it was okay for him to exclude her. Because she didn't like his reply, she punched him and told him he better never do it again.

At one point in the investigation, an adult pointed out to Monica that it was not okay to hit someone just because they make you mad. To this, Monica replied, "Well my mom says it is!" This was an "AH-HA" moment for the rest of us. We were reminded that not everyone plays by the same social rules. We live in a time where survival tactics are being taught, or caught, at home, without much thought about the rights of others. Not everyone is going to teach their children to be nice and respectful, and that it is wrong to make fun of others. Monica had been taught to dominate others before they could dominate her.

Walter was overweight. He had been most of his life. When he was younger, it was not as obvious. He could still participate in activities and he really wasn't teased about being a little larger than most of his classmates. However, as he entered his upper elementary years, his weight became more of a problem. Kids would chant, on a fairly regular basis, "Fatty, Fatty, 2 by 4, can't get through the bathroom door, so he did it on the floor!" They were relentless and mean. Walter was constantly reminded of his larger physique. He was not invited to the parties and was not asked to hang out after games. He was ostracized. Walter was alone.

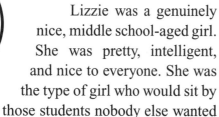

Lizzie was a genuinely nice, middle school-aged girl. She was pretty, intelligent, and nice to everyone. She was the type of girl who would sit by those students nobody else wanted to sit by. Some of the boys were starting to pay her attention, as well. Chansey, one of her classmates, did not like this. In fact, Chansey was jealous of Lizzie, and Lizzie's "nicey-nice" nature really rubbed her the wrong way. Unlike Lizzie, Chansey was more popular at this particular time because she was more athletic, more of a tomboy, and more outspoken, and had matured faster than Lizzie. Chansey was more of the "Leader of the Pack." Lizzie made Chansey look bad because Chansey wasn't nice to everyone and loved to talk behind her classmates' backs. Chansey would poison the water around her if given the chance. She decided to make sure Lizzie would be ridiculed and excluded. With this in mind, Chansey and some girls had a sleepover one night. It was the perfect opportunity for them to egg Lizzie's house.

It is 2000-something now and the stories still continue. We still have Maurices, Monicas, and Chanseys with us. The names and faces might have changed but the same bullying behaviors still exist. Just visit some social media sites, page through the local and national newspapers, or turn on the network news and you can read and hear about these types of incidences being played out on a regular basis across our country. Kids are targeted by other kids, and sadly even by adults, because they are physically different from other kids and act differently from their peers.

Unfortunately, the stakes have gotten higher in the last 30 years. In past years, you might have been bullied or teased at your school, and it was typically contained to just that one location. Today, when young people are targeted by others, they are targeted in front of the entire world, or in front of their entire world. The magnitude of ridicule has intensified to a point where we must educate students about and advocate for the victims of these social cruelties and crises.

For the purposes of this book, we will define bullying as "any behavior that threatens, intimidates, humiliates, or isolates a person or undermines their reputation or performance" (Fox S., & Stallworth, L.E., 2010). It can range from subtle slights to obvious and intentional emotional abuse, and it can be an isolated incident or occur frequently. Sometimes, it's nonverbal cues. The bullies' words may be fine, but the little things add up. These little things aren't in your face but they take place behind your back. Sometimes it's more blatant. It might be hostility toward another person or it could involve belittling, insulting, or putting someone down. It can involve yelling or cursing, spreading harmful rumors, or sabotaging someone's friends or activities. Isolation is another form of bullying. Detrimental actions include ignoring someone on Facebook or making false, malicious posts about them; excluding them from activities; giving them the silent treatment; intentionally leaving the room when someone enters; and failing to return their phone calls, emails, or texts. It can also involve sending others negative text messages about the person who is right there with the message sender.

Educating our youth about bullying is a start, but we must go beyond just having them recognize that intent and actions are harmful to others. We must connect with our youth and tap into their emotional world before we will see any kind of substantial change. Teaching youth positive social skills is one of the best ways to help them deal with intimidating, victimizing occurrences in their lives and the lives of their friends. They need help finding their "voice."

As long as there are humans, we will never totally eliminate bullying. But we can take steps to minimize it and the damage it leaves in its wake. With a focused effort, we can make a difference. The activities and ideas in this book may not eradicate bullying and benefit all youth, but they can help us help "just one child." By using these strategies and lessons, we can be somebody's "Difference"!

Fox, S., & Stallworth, L.E. (2010). The battered apple: An application of stressor-emotion-control/support theory to teachers' experience of violence and bullying. Human Relations, 63, 927-954. (Referenced in "Are You Being Bullied at Work by a Narcissist?" by Lisa Scott; www.lisaescott.com/forum/2011/.../are-you-being-bullied-work-narcissist)

The Unmasking

Secondary students are in a class all their own. Their hormones are raging. They want to fit in at all costs and they are fiercely loyal to their feelings and the feelings of others – at times, even at the expense of logic. They struggle with hygiene issues. Their curiosity can get the best of them, and they are trying to figure out who they are and where they belong. On top of this, all of these things are taking place in an emotional minefield. One wrong word or action, and the emotions can blow!

It is for these reasons that secondary students need opportunities to express who they are and what makes them tick. Letting them express themselves in safe environments provides adults with a better insight into their world and might give us clues as to why they act the way that they do. The activities in this book are designed to do just that. They are created with the middle school student in mind and they promote trying to hook into

their emotional mindset at this age. Healthy, honest communication is a foundational tool in bringing about change in our young people and in our schools.

You will find several lesson ideas in the following pages that are meant to deal directly with bullying and teasing. You can use these lessons as springboards for further lessons as well. Knowing that each classroom is unique and that each set of students comes with its own challenges, the lessons are designed with some flexibility, allowing you to change up the questions to better fit your students' needs.

Concepts Explored in Section 1:
- Who Am I?
- Greeting and Meeting Others
- Making and Choosing Friends

Who's Your Starfish?

OBJECTIVES:

Social Skill: Using the Starfish Story, students will learn strategies for appropriately approaching and greeting others.

Executive Function: Students will learn to promote social intelligence through successful interactions with other people.

MATERIALS NEEDED:

- Copy of the Starfish Story
- Starfish pattern (on CD)
- Pencil
- Markers (optional)
- Boys Town Social Skill "Greeting Others"

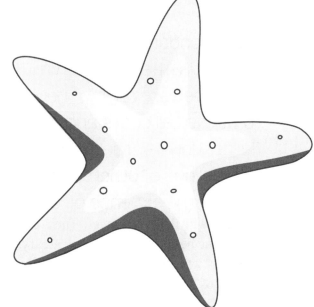

DIRECTIONS:

1. Have the class briefly research starfish, noting the typical size of starfish and how they get to the beach. Can they grow a new arm? How do they fit into the food chain? You can ask for other information as well.

2. Have each student cut out a starfish using the pattern.

3. Read the Starfish Story.

4. Have students discuss the meaning of the story and how it could relate to people they know or cross paths with during the course of a day.

5. Have each student think of one person who needs a friend or just needs to be included (like finding a starfish on the beach). With that person in mind, have each student give his starfish cut-out a "code" name so others won't know who that person is.

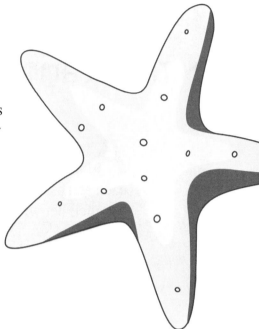

6. Ask students to write down five steps they could take to start being a friend to the person they have in mind, including how to approach and greet the person. Ask the students to write their lists on the back of their starfish cut-out, as well as on a piece of paper they can keep with them.

7. Discuss all suggestions and talk through which approaches and greetings might work best for different situations. Introduce the skill of **"Greeting Others,"** and discuss how to be socially "smart."

    a. *Make proper eye contact.*
    b. *Use a pleasant tone of voice.*
    c. *Say, "Hi" or "Hello."*

8. Give the students various scenarios and have them practice how to approach someone and greet him or her. Encourage all approaches and methods and let the class decide which ones they think will be most effective.

9. Have the students display their starfishes in the classroom. Advise them you will throw away one starfish each week unless they have saved it by doing one of the five things on their list. (Have the students let you know each time they use a step from their lists and initial their starfish to save it.)

Emphasizing different scenarios will give the students more ideas on how to feel socially successful and greet others in an appropriate way. Focus on body language, voice tone, eye contact, and word choice in order to promote higher social intelligence.

FLIPPED CLASSROOM SUGGESTIONS:

Post brief videos or lessons on starfish that students can view before class. Including a brief online quiz or activity will provide immediate feedback to determine if students have understood the material being presented. At the start of class, ask students for questions on the material they viewed.

The Starfish Story

A young girl was walking along a beach where thousands of starfish had been washed up during a terrible storm. As she came to each starfish, she picked it up and threw it back into the ocean. People watched her with amusement.

She had been doing this for some time when a man approached her and said, "Little girl, why are you doing this? Look at this beach! You can't save all these starfish. You can't begin to make a difference!"

The girl seemed suddenly deflated. But after a few moments, she bent down, picked up another starfish, and hurled it as far as she could into the ocean. Then she looked up at the man and replied,

"Well, I made a difference to that one!"

The old man looked at the girl inquisitively and thought about what she had done and said. Inspired, he joined the little girl in throwing starfish back into the sea. Soon others joined, and all the starfish were saved.

Adapted from *The Star Thrower* by Loren C. Eiseley

 From this perspective, we CAN help to change a life. We CAN help to change a mind. We CAN help change a circumstance. Our efforts CAN make a difference to "ONE"!

Behind the Mask

ACTIVITY 1

OBJECTIVES:

Social Skills: Students will learn and practice how to introduce themselves to someone else, which will help promote tolerance and acceptance of differences in others.

Executive Functions: Students will display self-confidence and the ability to control their emotions while presenting their masks.

MATERIALS NEEDED:

- A collection of masks
- "History of Masquerade Balls" question sheet on CD
- (Optional) Pictures of masquerade balls from various time periods
- Assorted paper
- Glue
- An assortment of arts and crafts supplies
- Scissors
- Paint
- Pencils
- Boys Town Social Skill "Introducing Yourself to Others"
- "Behind the Mask" grading rubric
- (Optional) Video or audio clip of the rock group The Who singing "Who Are You?"

DIRECTIONS:

1. Bring in several masks for the students to see, or view some on the Internet. Ask students about the types of masks they have worn before.

2. Explain how masks came into existence by giving the history of masquerade balls or parties, or by having the students use the Internet to explore the historical reasons for masks and masquerade balls.

3. After exploring the historical traditions of masks, have each student make his or her own mask. Students can use any media available to make their masks. Before they begin, tell the students that the masks must represent them and their values, and cannot just be any old mask that they think looks cool or is scary or gross.

4. Have each student list six ways her mask represents her while completing the activity.

5. Introduce the skill of **"Introducing Yourself to Others"**:

   a. *Look at the person. Smile.*

   b. *Use a pleasant voice.*

   c. *Offer a greeting. Say, "Hi, my name is…."*

   d. *In a one-on-one or small group setting, shake the person's hand. In a large group setting, wave or give some other sign of positive recognition.*

   e. *As you end the conversation, say, "It was nice to meet you," or something similar.*

6. Have students display and talk about their masks with the class, explaining why it represents them. As part of this sharing, students must properly and confidently introduce themselves to the class. Give students a copy of the grading rubric at the end of the section and have them use it to grade the mask presentations. Also have students complete a rubric on their own presentation so they can gauge whether or not they were in control of their emotions.

7. After everyone has presented their masks, hold a class discussion on masks. Ask students to write down their answers to the following questions on the activity sheet and then discuss:

   a. Historically, why did people wear masks?

   b. What advantage would there have been to wearing a mask?

   c. Can you think of ways in which our society wears masks?

   d. When do people wear masks?

   e. When have you worn a mask?

   f. Are you wearing one now?

   g. Is your mask similar to anyone else's?

   h. Do you think bullies hide behind a mask?

   i. Do you think victims hide behind a mask?

   j. Do we always know who the bullies are?

   k. Do we always know who the victims are?

   l. Can bullies and victims fool and deceive us?

   m. Why do bullies and victims hide behind masks?

   n. How can we show that we are tolerant and accepting of another person's differences?

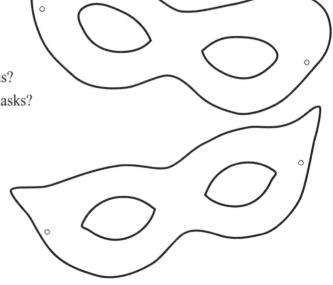

8. (Optional) If possible, play a video clip of the The Who singing their 1978 hit, "Who Are You?" Just show the first several seconds of the song so students can hear the lyrics, "Who are you? Who, who, who, who," several times. Then turn off the video and challenge them with... "WHO ARE YOU REALLY?"

Allow students time to really process the design of their masks. You want them to start thinking about who they really are.

FLIPPED CLASSROOM SUGGESTIONS:

On a class blog, post historical information about masks and links to videos depicting the historical significance of wearing one. Ask students to post their thoughts on the topic to the blog. Review the blog and the students' responses in class and carry on the discussion and activities from there.

Use the Internet for educational purposes and get permission to use sites that require it.

ADDITIONAL RESOURCES:

http://www.historyofmasks.net/
https://en.wikipedia.org/wiki/Masquerade_ball

Behind the Mask Rubric

	YES	NO
Did the student look at the class?	○	○
Did the student smile?	○	○
Did the student use a pleasant voice?	○	○
Did the student have appropriate posture while introducing himself or herself?	○	○
Did the student offer a greeting, such as, "Hi, my name is…"?	○	○
Did the student speak and act confidently?	○	○
Was the student able to control his or her emotions by not exhibiting fear, nervousness, embarrassment, goofiness, or arrogance?	○	○

Explain. _____

Behind the Mask – A C T I V I T Y 1

Write down answers to the questions below.

1. Historically, why did people wear masks?_____
    _____

2. What advantage would there have been to wearing a mask? _____
    _____
    _____
    _____

3. Can you think of ways in which our society wears masks?_____
    _____
    _____

4. When do people wear masks? _____
    _____

5. When have you worn a mask?_____
    _____

6. Are you wearing one now?_____
    _____
    _____

7. Is your mask similar to anyone else's? _____
    _____
    _____
    _____

8. Do you think bullies hide behind a mask? _____

_____

_____

9. Do you think victims hide behind a mask? _____

_____

_____

10. Do we always know who the bullies are? _____

_____

_____

11. Do we always know who the victims are? _____

_____

_____

12. Can bullies and victims fool and deceive us? _____

_____

_____

13. Why do bullies and victims hide behind masks? _____

_____

_____

14. How can we show that we are tolerant and accepting of another person's differences? _____

_____

_____

_____

Behind the Mask

ACTIVITY 2

OBJECTIVES:

Social Skills: Students will review the skill of "Introducing Yourself to Others" and exhibit ways they can be tolerant of other people's differences.

Executive Functions: Students will work to display optimism about their future as seen through the portrayal of their second mask. They will work toward showing zest for the activity.

MATERIALS NEEDED:

- Assorted paper
- Glue
- Scissors
- An assortment of arts and crafts supplies
- Paint
- Boys Town Social Skill "Introducing Yourself to Others"
- Rubric from the previous "Behind the Mask" activity

DIRECTIONS:

1. After the class has completed the first "Behind the Mask" activity, ask the students to create a second mask. This time, however, have them make a mask of who they want to be. You could put the emphasis either on who they want to be right now or who they want to be in five years. Remind students that possessing zest means that they actively participate in and show enthusiasm for an activity.

2. Once the students have made their second mask, ask them to share their masks with the class, explaining how it relates to them. Remind them of the social skill, "Introducing Yourself to Others," and the rubric they will be using.

3. After all the students have shared their masks, have them write down answers to the following questions on the activity sheet:

   a. Are your two masks different? If so, how? Why?

   b. If they are the same in any way, why did you keep them the same?

   c. Would you like someone else's mask?

   d. Do you think your mask will change in the future?

e.   Do you think you will ever be totally rid of your mask? Why or why not?

f.   How can we feel more at ease about just being ourselves?

g.   If you don't like your mask or how it portrays you in the future, can you change it?

h.   How can you show appreciation and respect for other people's masks or for them as individuals?

ANSWER: *Allow them to be who they want.*

4.   Have students share their answers. While they are doing this, get them to the point where they realize that through effort, they can change their future and their intellect and character in ways that will improve their future. They also can allow other people to be who they want to be without fear of being embarrassed or bullied.

Emphasize the fact that through effort, students CAN change and improve their intellect and their character. This, in turn, will help them to better succeed in the future. Also, place importance on allowing others to be who they really want to be and to be accepted for that.

FLIPPED CLASSROOM SUGGESTIONS:

Instead of asking the questions under No. 3 in the classroom, post them to a class blog and ask each student to post his or her answers by a class number instead of a name. They could also email their answers. Another suggestion would be to have students videotape themselves covering the topic of optimism in regard to their future and how they have the power to change. They would then come to class and work on their masks and write the answers to the questions.

ADDITIONAL RESOURCES:

Rubric from the first "Behind the Mask'" activity

NAME:_____

Behind the Mask - ACTIVITY 2

Write down answers to the questions below.

1. Are your two masks different? If so, how? Why? _____
    _____
    _____

2. If they are the same in any way, why did you keep them the same? _____
    _____
    _____

3. Would you like someone else's mask?_____

4. Do you think your mask will change in the future? _____
    _____

5. Do you think you will ever be totally rid of your mask? Why or why not?_____
    _____

6. How can we feel more at ease about just being ourselves? _____
    _____

7. If you don't like your mask or how it portrays you in the future, can you change it?
    _____
    _____

8. How can you show appreciation and respect for other people's masks or for them as
    individuals? _____
    _____

Cliques

OBJECTIVES:

Social Skills: Students will increase their understanding of why it is important to include others and make many friends.

Executive Functions: Students will demonstrate flexibility when encountering artificial impediments while running the obstacle course and will run the race with zest despite the restrictions.

MATERIALS NEEDED:

- Ideas/Materials for constructing an obstacle course for student teams to run
- Blindfolds, headsets, tape, and string
- Stopwatch
- Backpack
- Heavy books
- Other items to add to the backpack
- Copies of "What Middle Schoolers Do"
- Paper
- Pencil
- Boys Town Social Skill "Making New Friends"

Cliques have been around for hundreds of years and I'm pretty sure they will continue. I don't think we will ever do away with them, but we can help to minimize their negative effects and the stereotypes that surround them. Cliques start out with those individuals who have something in common. They share interests or their personalities just mesh really well, and they feel supported and valued by each other. Somewhere along the line, this group of individuals turns into an exclusive group. The individuals in the clique don't see the value or worth of others outside of their group. They feel superior to others, and at times, inferior.

DIRECTIONS:

1. Prior to class, set up an obstacle course for students to run. Divide the students into teams or have them partner up, taking care to separate students who normally would want to be together.

2. Let each team run the obstacle course one time, and time how long it takes them.

3. Tell each team they will run the course again, but this time they will be tasked with the following hardships:

   - Some teams cannot use one or both of their legs
   - Some teams cannot use one or both of their arms
   - Some teams have to wear headsets so team members can't hear each other
   - Some teams must wear blindfolds so they can't see (except for one member of the group)
   - Some teams cannot talk at all

4. Time each group as they run the obstacle course the second time and compare their two times.

5. Change hardships for teams and have them run the obstacle course again, again timing them. Check for enthusiastic participation and possibly give a prize to the most enthusiastic team/ student.

6. Discuss how running the obstacle course with all our abilities is much easier than running it without certain abilities.

7. Relate this discussion to how schools, communities, and society work better and more efficiently when all members are valued for their contributions as well as their differences. People need to be able to think and act differently in order for society to progress and thrive. We should celebrate our differences and value all people.

8. Have students read the poem "What Middle Schoolers Do." In groups of four, have students write down what they think the poem means.

9. Have someone read the poem aloud to the class. Discuss. Ask students if they have friends like those described in the poem. If so, ask them how they can make new friends?

10. Introduce the skill of **"Making New Friends"**:

    a. *Find a potential new friend and pleasantly introduce yourself.*

    b. *Share some of your interest and hobbies.*

    c. *Listen to the other person's name and interests.*

    d. *Plan some activities with the person, with permission.*

11. Ask for a student volunteer to come to the front and put on an empty backpack. Ask the other students if this would be hard to carry around. Tell them this is like the start of the school year; everyone is usually excited and pretty carefree about the upcoming year.

12. Start adding things to the backpack. Add a heavy book and tell the students that it represents not being able to sit at a particular lunch table. Another added book might represent someone laughing at them or gossiping about them. A heavy dictionary might symbolize being told they were going to get "beat up." After you have added several items, ask the students if this would be burdensome to carry around now. Tell them that many of them are carrying around a backpack like this right now. They might have been excluded or laughed at. They might have been verbally or physically "beat up." Or, their backpack might be heavy with guilt or pressure.

13. Relate how carrying all this weight can wear on the students and change their outlook. Some students might feel like giving up or just not coming to school. Ask them what they can do about this.

    ANSWER: *Find ways to take out some of the weight! They don't have to let cliques or bullies run their social life. If they lighten their load each day, they will find that over time, they will be happier and more confident in advocating for themselves. They can accept more people and have more friends who can enrich their life.*

On the obstacle course, be sure to include some obstacles that have to be thrown or lifted. Students should have to perform these tasks together and they should not be easy for any team unless they can use all of their physical abilities.

FLIPPED CLASSROOM SUGGESTIONS:

Post the poem "What Middle Schoolers Do" online to your website or blog. Have students read the poem and write down what they think it means on a piece of paper. This will be their "ticket" into class the next day. Also, post a short video on cliques and what students can do about them.

Have the students run the obstacle course and backpack activities during class and elaborate on the meanings of the activities.

What Middle Schoolers Do

A shake of the head, a roll of the eyes

The rumors, the lies

They no longer play on your pride

But rip you up inside

This is what Middle Schoolers do

This is what they say

It is like this every day

The mothers reply

But that is a lie

Walking in the hall

Taking in it all

All alone no one home

Kids shouting, kids staring

All this torture I'm bearing

No one caring.

– Anonymous, Age 12

Not So Smooth

OBJECTIVES:

Social Skills: Students will explore the ways and advantages of choosing appropriate friends.

Executive Functions: This activity promotes the development of social intelligence among students.

MATERIALS NEEDED:

- A sheet of wax paper for each student
- Boys Town Social Skill "Choosing Appropriate Friends"

DIRECTIONS:

1. Give each student a piece of wax paper to play with. (This represents them going about their everyday life.)

2. Ask the students to wad up their piece of wax paper as they think of someone who has made them mad or who they don't like very much. Tell the students they can think of things they would say to that person as they continue to wad the wax paper.

3. Next, ask students to straighten their wax paper until there are no wrinkles or lines in it. (This will not be possible.) Encourage them to really try to get it as smooth as it was at the start of the activity.

4. Ask students how this relates to bullying.

The words we say to other people, or the looks we give them, or the way we exclude them can cause irreversible damage to another person, just like the irreversible damage you caused to the wax paper. You can get your wax paper smoother but you can't get rid of all the lines and wrinkles. Similarly, you can apologize to another person and really mean it, but you can't totally erase the words from that other person's mind.

5. Ask students to share a time when someone said or did something hurtful to them.

6. Have students brainstorm ways that they can find good friends, how and when they can include others, and how they can find solutions during conflicts with others. Use the following **"Choosing Appropriate Friends"** steps as a guide:

   a. *Think of the qualities and interests you want in a friend.*

   b. *Look at the strengths and weaknesses of potential friends.*

   c. *Match your interests and activities with those of potential friends.*

   d. *Avoid peers who are involved with bullying, drugs, gangs, or illegal activities.*

7. Have students write their ideas on a large piece of paper that you can display in the classroom.

. . . .

TIPS Remind students not to use the names of other people when they are sharing personal experiences.

. . . .

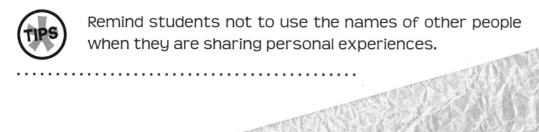

Recognizing the Labels

Before students can take a stand against bullying they must be able to identify what it is they are standing against. Many students will have a good idea of what bullying is, in the broad sense of the word. But they will need practice and the opportunities to uncover the true faces of bullying. We want them to know what bullying looks like in "their" world. When a youth can uncover the faces of bullying, it becomes a little less intimidating and we have a better chance of propelling students into taking a stand against the injustices bullying causes. Recognizing the labels they place on their peers will help them navigate the steps needed to better see and tolerate the

differences in others. This will help them see the need to become the difference in the life of "one."

Concepts Explored in Section 2:
- Tolerating Others
- Identifying Bullies and Victims
- Communicating with Others

The Bullying of Different Types of Students

OBJECTIVES:

Social Skills: Students will learn the skill of "Tolerating Differences in Others" and how to generalize it to different types of people.

Executive Functions: Students will exercise social intelligence by understanding and respecting that other people are not the same as they are.

MATERIALS NEEDED:

- Pictures of and questions about several different types of bullying victims
- Access to computers
- Action Plan form
- Boys Town Social Skill "Tolerating Differences in Others"
- Paper
- Pencil

There seems to be "types" of students who are more at risk of being bullied and "types" of students who are more likely to do the bullying. Most of us could identify these "types," even in our workplace and the social arenas of our adult lives. This has been going on for decades. The names have changed, but the victims and bullies may eerily resemble those we knew when we were in our middle school years. Students can usually identify these two classifications in others but have more difficulty identifying them in themselves or a close friend.

DIRECTIONS:

1. Browse the Internet for pictures of various "types" of bullying that occur frequently in your school. Save these on your computer or print off copies and laminate them. You also could save the images to a blog/website.

2. Use the images as picture prompts. Project each picture onto your board through your computer. Pause for several minutes on each one and ask the students to write a caption for the picture.

3. Collect the captions after you have gone through all the images.

4. Go back through the images and discuss each picture while reading a few randomly selected captions you collected from the students for that picture.

5. Ask students questions about the pictures. The questions you ask will depend on the pictures you used, but they might sound like this:

   a. Why do you think this group is making fun of someone who dresses differently and wears glasses?

   b. Why does the boy have his head buried in his hands?

   c. Why are these students just standing there looking at the person who is by himself?

6. Question the students about how the bullies or bystanders in these pictures could be more tolerant of the victim or others who are different from them.

7. Review the steps of the skill of **"Tolerating Differences in Others"**:

   a. *Think about the similarities you share with the other person.*

   b. *Take note of your differences.*

   c. *Emphasize what you have in common* (interests, activity, etc.)

   d. *Express respect or appreciation for the person.*

If you have students post their picture captions to a class website or blog, make sure you review and approve them before they are displayed. Remember that, ultimately, you are trying to visually identify the types of bullying that occur, whether they are physical, verbal, mental, or sexual, and to identify what bullying might look like. You also are trying to point out several types of "victims." When students can recognize stereotypes and bullying behaviors, they can better identify what to do to "be the difference."

FLIPPED CLASSROOM SUGGESTIONS:

Post several pictures of bullying to your website/blog. Have students write captions for each one and bring them to class. Have students write action plans for each picture, in groups, during class time.

ADDITIONAL RESOURCES:

Conduct an Internet search for bullying pictures. Always make sure you include site addresses/permission when using the images.

www.safetyweb.com

Action Plan Form

Write down answers to the below questions after viewing the selected pictures.

1. Visually identify the type(s) of bullying that is occurring (i.e., physical, verbal, mental, or sexual)._____

   _____

   _____

   _____

2. What does the bully look like to you? _____

   _____

   _____

3. Who is the victim and how would you describe him or her?_____

   _____

   _____

4. How does the ability to describe the type of bullying that is occurring and the victims help you better identify when bullying is occurring? _____

   _____

   _____

5. What can you do to "be the difference" when you see bullying occurring? _____

   _____

   _____

Behind the Mask:
Who Are You?

A C T I V I T Y   3

OBJECTIVES:

Social Skills: Students will actively participate in the activities, showing tolerance of others' differences.

Executive Functions: Students will display zest throughout the activity, practicing self-control and social intelligence as labels are placed on various classmates.

MATERIALS NEEDED:

- Labels for students, either a sign they can stick to their back or a headband (see template on CD)
- Paper
- Pencil
- Boys Town Social Skill "Tolerating Differences in Others"

DIRECTIONS:

1. Make signs or labels that describe what students or people in general may be known as. Some can be negative and some can be positive. Some possible names to use include:

   - flirt
   - geek
   - jock
   - smart
   - gamer
   - nice
   - prep
   - loser
   - ditsy
   - musical
   - hipster
   - granola
   - dummy
   - athletic
   - gangbanger
   - class clown

ditsy   **gamer**   **hipster**

2. Put a sign on each student's back or put a headband on their head, making sure the person who is wearing the label can't see it. (Be very careful not to set up a situation for actual bullying to occur in the classroom. For example, if you have a student who is particularly smart, labeling him or her as the "geek" may open the door for actual class-approved bullying.)

3. Remind the students that the labels are just for this activity and do not really represent the person who is wearing the label.

4. Review the definition of "stereotype."

5. Ask the students to come up to the front of the room one at a time. Then have the rest of the class start talking to the person the way they would if they really felt that person was what the label said.

6. After several minutes of treating the student according to his or her label, ask that student to tell what it felt like and what he or she thinks the label says.

7. If some students try to be funny or dominate the activity, politely remind them to allow others to have a turn and to use a normal and pleasant tone of voice. Check for interrupting as well.

8. Look for students who demonstrate respect for other students' statements and feelings about the labels. Verbally praise them.

9. Ask the students why it was so easy to think of things to say to the individuals with these labels.

10. Ask the students if a person is ever mistakenly labeled or if it is hard to get rid of a label once you have it. Ask how that relates to our identities.

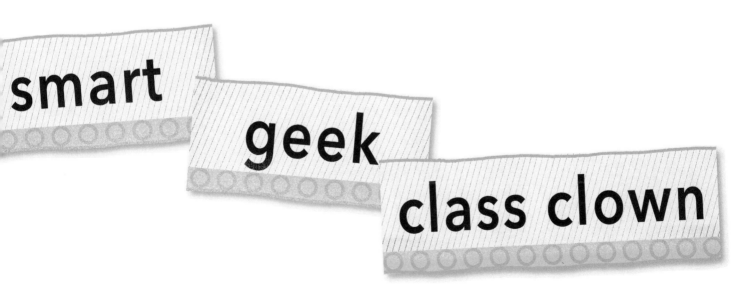

11. Review the steps of the skill of **"Tolerating Differences in Others"**:

    a. *Think about the similarities you share with the other person.*

    b. *Take note of your differences.*

    c. *Emphasize what you have in common* (interests, activity, etc.).

    d. *Express respect or appreciation for the person.*

12. (Optional) Have all students take a look at their label and offer a better way someone could have addressed them during the activity (a way that demonstrated tolerance for differences). This could be done in a written format or verbally, or you could have the class pair-share.

 The labels might need to be changed according to the issues you face in your classroom and school.

The Pot Stirrers
ACTIVITY 1

OBJECTIVES:

Social Skills: Students will practice apologizing to another person.

Executive Functions: Social intelligence will be on display as students show respect for others by practicing apologies.

MATERIALS NEEDED:

- Can of Silly String®
- Paper
- Pencil
- Boys Town Social Skill "Making an Apology"

"Pot Stirrers" are the gossips. They thrive on the drama of teen life. They love to get the juicy gossip flowing. If there isn't any drama, they create it. They usually start it and then just sit back and watch the show. "Pot Stirrers" are difficult to catch.

DIRECTIONS:

1. Explain the old game of "Telephone" to students and then play it.

2. Discuss how the initial statement whispered in the first person's ear is different from the statement the last person heard (including times when students weren't sure what they heard or were trying to be funny).

3. Ask students the following questions:

   a. Has this ever happened to them?

   b. Are there people who love to embellish, exaggerate, and falsify information?

   c. Why is this and what do we call people like that?

   d. How is gossip like the "Telephone" game?

4. Write the following statement on the board and ask students what it means: "He who gossips with you will gossip of you."

5. Start the Silly String Activity. Begin by saying negative things about fictitious characters, such as movie characters or animated characters. Spray the Silly String each time you say something negative. Have the students take turns as well. Point out that many students are having fun but others look a little uncomfortable. Ask students if they think some people feel bad after they say something mean about someone else, and wish they could take it back.

6. Relate gossip to the Silly String by asking the students to put the Silly String back in the can. Of course, they won't be able to, so point out how we can never take back the words we say.

7. Ask what they could do if they have said something hurtful and wished that they wouldn't have.

    ANSWER: *Apologize*

8. Go over the skill of **"Making an Apology."**

    a. *Look the other person in the eye.*

    b. *Use a sincere voice.*

    c. *Be direct and say, "I'm sorry."*

    d. *Don't make excuses or blame someone else.*

    e. *Let the person know how you might change in the future.*

    f. *Thank the person for listening.*

9. Have students practice apologizing in groups of two.

10. Finally, ask what they should do if someone does not apologize.

· ·

Write down negative things to say about fictitious characters before class. Write some down for the students to say as well.

· ·

Apologizing 1, 2, 3, 4

OBJECTIVES:

Social Skills: Students will effectively practice the steps of the skills of "Making an Apology" and "Accepting an Apology."

Executive Functions: Students will understand that it takes emotional control to effectively apologize and a degree of optimism to accept an apology.

MATERIALS NEEDED:

- Paper
- Pencil
- (Optional) Access to a computer

- Boys Town Social Skill "Making an Apology"
- Boys Town Social Skill "Accepting an Apology"

 At times throughout our lives we find ourselves in situations where we have caused others turmoil or harm. Learning how to sincerely apologize is part of maturing and taking responsibility for one's own words and actions. We can make students apologize to other students, but only true, heartfelt apologies can bring about positive change in behavior. It seems that there are four main ways students typically apologize.

1. **"Caught Red-Handed"**

   This type of apology is made out of guilt. The person has been caught red-handed and is forced to apologize. It is usually very quick and non-emotional, and involves a mumbled "Sorry."

2. **"One & Done"**

   The person at fault apologizes very quickly but not with much feeling. The person acknowledges he or she is at fault because his or her conscience is trained to realize the fault, but it is a rote kind of apology. This is the quick "Sorry" you say as you continue to cut in front of someone. You know it is not the nicest thing, so you say "Sorry," but continue with your actions anyway.

3. "I'm Sorry, But…."

The person who uses this type of apology acknowledges that he or she is at fault, but justifies his or her actions by pointing out somebody else's wrong behaviors. The person passes the buck, diverting attention away from his or her wrong actions.

4. "If The Shoe Fits…"

This is a sincere, heartfelt apology. The person states that the incident was his or her fault and is remorseful for the action. This is the only apology that is genuine and brings about change. It is a sign of emotional maturity.

DIRECTIONS:

1. Review the four types of apologies with students.

2. Ask how a person genuinely apologizes. After getting input from students, introduce the skill of **"Making an Apology"**:

   a. *Look the other person in the eye (can't be done by email, text, or a note).*

   b. *Use a sincere voice.*

   c. *Be direct and say, "I'm sorry."*

   d. *Don't make excuses or blame someone else.*

   e. *Let the person know how you might change in the future.*

   f. *Thank the person for listening.*

3. Explain how the offended person also needs to accept the apology, and introduce the skill of **"Accepting an Apology"**:

   a. *Look at the person who is apologizing.*

   b. *Listen to what the person is saying.*

   c. *Remain calm.*

   d. *Thank the person for the apology.*

4. Have students write their own versions of the four types of apologies, making sure they include at least one example of a time when they used each of the four types. They also should include the strategies for making an effective apology.

5. An alternative to having students write their own versions of the four apologies would be to have them create posters on http://edu.glogster.com. You can sign up for a free account there and create posters online.

· ·

 Creating and keeping the posters under the teacher's login is easier to manage. (Just be sure to change your password after completing the activity.)

· ·

FLIPPED CLASSROOM SUGGESTIONS:

Post the four types of apologies and the effective ways to apologize and accept an apology online through your website or blog, or on videotape. After students gather the necessary information, have them sign up for Glogster (through your account or on their own) and begin making their posters.

During class time, discuss the apologies and have students continue working on their posters.

The Pot Stirrers
ACTIVITY 2

OBJECTIVES:

Social Skills: Students will learn the differences between gossip and communicating honestly.

Executive Functions: Students will explore the differences between integrity and gossip.

MATERIALS NEEDED:

- Paper
- Pencil
- (Optional) Access to computers
- Copy of the poem, "Gossip"
- Boys Town Social Skill "Communicating Honestly"

DIRECTIONS:

1. Have students read the "Gossip" poem.

2. Have students write their reactions to the poem and share them with the class.

3. Ask students to write their own poem about gossip.

4. Display or post poems on the class website/blog.

5. Ask students how gossip differs from honesty and integrity.

6. Review how someone would answer and treat someone honestly by introducing the social skill of **"Communicating Honestly."**

   a. *Look at the person.*

   b. *Use a clear voice.*

   c. *Respond to questions factually and completely.*

   d. *Don't leave out important details or facts.*

   e. *With integrity, take responsibility for your actions.*

7. Ask students to write their own poem about honesty and integrity, or have them write a poem contrasting gossip with honesty and genuineness.

 This activity would complement a poetry unit very well by having students write their poem in a particular poetic format.

FLIPPED CLASSROOM SUGGESTIONS:

Record yourself reading the "Gossip" poem and post it on your class website or blog. Students can listen to the poem and write their reactions before coming to class. During class time, help students write their own poems.

○ ○ ○ Gossip

My name is Gossip.

I have no respect for justice.

I maim without killing.

I break hearts and ruin lives.

I am cunning and malicious and gather strength with age.

The more I am quoted, the more I am believed.

I flourish at every level of society.

My victims are helpless.

They cannot protect themselves against me because
      I have no name and no face.

To track me down is impossible.

The harder you try, the more elusive I become.

I am nobody's friend.

Once I tarnish a reputation, it is never quite the same.

My name is Gossip.

– Author Unknown

Valuing Others

One of the goals in education is to empower our youth to be productive, successful individuals in our society. We want them to possess confidence in themselves and in their unique abilities and talents, so they can contribute to our communities in a meaningful and beneficial way. With this in mind, encouraging students to value themselves as well as the uniqueness of others puts into motion this higher calling.

Showing empathy for others, valuing and using the differences in others to springboard into greater tasks, and learning from and disagreeing with others are attributes that will help students feel more comfortable in taking a stand for what they believe. It is through these attributes that they can learn to respect the viewpoints of others while developing the skills they need to get along in the world.

When students can value others without losing themselves, change CAN happen.

Concepts Explored in Section 3:
- Valuing Differences
- Empathy for Others
- Disagreeing Appropriately

That's Me... Or Not

ACTIVITY 1

OBJECTIVES:

Social Skills: Students will practice how to disagree appropriately. They will also work together with a team to support their point of view.

Executive Functions: Students will practice showing zest through active participation, self-control by allowing others to speak without interrupting, and curiosity by actively listening to others and answering or asking questions at the appropriate time to further their understanding.

MATERIALS NEEDED:

- "That's Me" and "Not For Me" signs (See resources)
- List of statements to use during the debate
- Historical information on debates
- Visual for the Boys Town Social Skill "Disagreeing Appropriately"

DIRECTIONS:

1. Define and briefly discuss what a debate is and when they typically are used (e.g., presidential debates on television, high school debate teams, debating with parents or friends).

2. During this discussion, lay the ground rules for the debate:

   a. You will read a statement, and after the students hear it, they will have to decide whether it reflects their beliefs or not. Depending on what they decide, students will go stand under either the "That's Me" or "Not For Me" sign you have hung on the wall.

   b. After everyone has picked a side, you will randomly select two students from each side to be the debaters for that statement. The rest of the students for each team (side) will circle around the debaters and give them ideas that will help them defend their viewpoint. Point out that working with others requires discussing ideas in a calm, quiet voice and letting everyone share their ideas.

c. Allow the teams to collaborate for a few minutes and then ask the debaters to come to the center of the room. The debaters should face each other and the other students should sit with their team. Remind the other students that they are not allowed to comment during the debate but will have a chance to offer input at the end. For now, they should really listen to what is being said and think of any questions or comments they might have.

d. Tell the debaters to start debating their side of the statement, taking turns at speaking and not interrupting when someone else is speaking. You also will review the steps to the skill of **"Disagreeing Appropriately."**

1. *Look at the person.*
2. *Use a pleasant voice.*
3. *Say, "I understand how you feel."*
4. *Tell why you feel differently.*
5. *Give a reason.*
6. *Listen to the other person.*

e. You also will remind the students that they are not debating you. They will want approval from you, but you should remain quiet and neutral at this point.

3. To begin the debate, read the statement again and have the debaters start debating. Once you feel they are finished, ask for input from the other students. Don't respond to their statements at this point; just let them voice their opinions.

4. Finally, point out a few positives and negatives for both sides to give students some "food for thought." You may have more positives for one side, or you might simply state, "The majority of you thought…."

5. Ask students if anyone was convinced to change sides because of what was said during the debate.

- -

We want to send the message to students that they should allow others to be who they are, and they should be okay with that. We want to see emotion from students. Youth are good at giving you the answer they think you want to hear. This activity is designed to expose their more genuine emotions and thoughts through their viewpoints on social issues.

- -

After the students have selected a side, it can prove beneficial to point out what the majority of students believe. To get them to be themselves, you can joke with them that there are no hidden cameras so their parents won't ever see the debate. This usually gets students to relax. Change the list of statements to fit the issues your students might face or have experience with.

FLIPPED CLASSROOM SUGGESTIONS:

Post a video of an actual debate on the class website for students to view before coming to class. Tell them to be ready to list a few other types of debates and the etiquette that is followed during a debate.

ADDITIONAL RESOURCES:

Video of a presidential debate or high school debate program.

"That's Me... Or Not"
Debate Statements

1. A person's appearance is a good indicator of what's inside.

2. I am entitled to act the way I want.

3. Bullying and teasing is the same thing.

4. Some people do things that make them easier to bully.

5. If you disagree with someone, you should just fight it out.

6. It is okay to lie to your parents.

7. Everyone should be able to do whatever they want without getting into trouble.

8. Teasing is not a big deal.

9. If a girl really likes a boy, she should be willing to do whatever he wants.

10. It is okay for teenagers to lie to each other.

11. It is okay for a person to do nothing while the National Anthem is being sung or the Pledge of Allegiance is being recited.

12. Teenagers should have the right to put whatever they want on Facebook.

13. If you have a problem with someone, it doesn't really do any good to talk about it.

14. Society makes too big of a deal about bullying.

15. Smoking makes you look cool and mature.

16. I can make a difference against bullying.

17. It is perfectly okay for teenagers to talk about other people behind their back.

18. Calling someone a name is not a big deal.

19. Everyone bears some responsibility for making our society work.

20. People should be able to put whatever they want on the Internet.

That's Me... or Not

ACTIVITY 2

> **OBJECTIVES:**
>
> **Social Skills:** Students will review how to appropriately disagree with someone.
>
> **Executive Functions:** Students will use self-control skills by paying attention, not interrupting, and getting to work right away.

MATERIALS NEEDED:

- Paper
- Pencil
- Boys Town Social Skill "Disagreeing Appropriately"
- Possible access to computers

DIRECTIONS:

1. Review the first "That's Me... Or Not" activity.

2. Ask students the following questions:

   a. What makes it easy or difficult to agree with someone?

   b. Do you disagree with your friends differently from how you disagree with a brother or sister? (Ask for examples.)

   c. Do you disagree with a teacher differently from how you disagree with a parent? Why?

   d. If we don't agree with someone, what is the best way to disagree? (Ask students to make a list of ideas and share them.)

3. Review the "Disagreeing Appropriately" visual. Ask students how this type of disagreeing might work better than being sassy, giving attitude, becoming angry, or yelling.

4. Have students apply these techniques in a pretend bullying situation. Ask students to create their own cartoon of how this might look. They can use paper and pencil, or create cartoons online (if computers are available). Remind the students that even though these are cartoons, they should still send a serious message.

5. Review the expectations for self-control with the students before beginning the activity (pay attention, wait your turn, don't interrupt, stay on task).

Emphasize how the skill of "Disagreeing Appropriately" should be used in all the scenarios.

FLIPPED CLASSROOM SUGGESTIONS:

Have students view an online visual of the skill of "Disagreeing Appropriately" and come to class with a list of examples for how they disagree differently with some people.

ADDITIONAL RESOURCES:

Visit www.toondoo.com or other similar sites and create a teacher account. Then share the login and password information with students so they can create and keep all of their cartoons in one location, saving you time later. Be sure to change your password when the activity is completed.

Dear...

OBJECTIVES:

Social Skills: Students will practice expressing empathy toward others.

Executive Functions: Students will learn how to give good advice to others while practicing open-mindedness.

MATERIALS NEEDED:

- Paper
- Pencil
- Historical information on "Dear Abby"
- Copy of "Dear Victim"
- Boys Town Social Skill "Expressing Empathy and Understanding for Others"

DIRECTIONS:

1. Discuss historical and present-day communication methods and how they differ (Pony Express, Morse code, telegrams, letters, emails, Instagrams, Facebook, telephone, cell phone, Twitter).

2. Lead students to the realization that some forms of communication allow for the display of more emotions, while others allow for information to be transmitted within seconds. Stress that there are advantages to both, but that it is important to identify what message we are trying to send to someone before we can be sure of which form of communication to use. (No matter the type of communication, our words are powerful.)

3. Ask students for examples of times when they responded too quickly or too harshly to someone. (Eventually, get to the conclusion that unless we think about what we are going to say or do ahead of time, things often get worse or don't come out the way we want. In fact, we can become a victim of somebody's words, or we can make someone else a victim by our own words.)

4. Tell students about "Dear Abby." (She was a columnist that gave people advice based on their situations and the questions they asked her. If possible, provide examples of some of her columns for students to review.)

5. Introduce the skill of **"Expressing Empathy and Understanding for Others"**:

    a. *Listen closely as the other person expresses his or her feelings.*

    b. *Express empathy by saying, "I understand...."*

    c. *Demonstrate concern through your words and actions.*

    d. *Reflect back the other person's words by saying, "It seems like you're saying...."*

    e. *Offer any help or assistance you can.*

6. Have students read the "Dear Victim" quote at the end of this section.

7. Have students respond to the quote by writing a letter to the victim, explaining what the quote means and how they might use the skill of "Expressing Empathy and Understanding for Others" in this situation. Have them imagine that the person they are writing to is a victim of either someone's harsh words, name-calling, teasing, bullying, or abuse.

8. Remind students to approach the assignment with empathy for the victim, and with wisdom and an open mind.

· ·

Relate the activity back to bullying and observe those who tend to be involved in the activity on a personal level.

· ·

FLIPPED CLASSROOM SUGGESTIONS:

Post a video on many forms of communication. Ask the students to watch the video and write down which methods they felt provided the most personal interaction and feeling. Also have them determine if speed of response is always a positive thing. Then, during class, help the students with their responses, challenging them to really understand the victim quote and to give wise advice to the victim.

○ ○ ○ ## Dear Victim,

Feelings are much like waves.

We can't stop them from coming, but

We can choose which ones to surf.

– By Jonatan Martensson

Let It Be

> **OBJECTIVES:**
>
> **Social Skills:** Students will explore the value of tolerating differences in others.
>
> **Executive Functions:** Students will write down ways they are respecting the feelings of others and displaying better social intelligence.

MATERIALS NEEDED:

- Paper
- Pencil
- Vis a Vis markers
- Boys Town Social Skill "Tolerating Differences in Others"

- "Let It Be" board (This is a long piece of butcher paper displayed somewhere in the room. Choose a width that can go through a laminator and a surface that allows students to write messages and erase them so they can post different messages throughout the school year.)

DIRECTIONS:

1. For best results, use this activity on a day you are returning a graded quiz to students.

2. As students enter the classroom, have them put all their things in one pile.

3. Tell them they will now live in a world of "same." This means that anyone can use anything that belongs to someone else (e.g., notebooks, pencils, purses, etc.). Really exaggerate and emphasize this, but don't let students actually take anything from another student at this point; just let them complain and question you.

4. Pass back a quiz or something else with a grade on it. Beforehand, put students' actual quiz grades on their papers, but strike through them and put the same, lower score on all the papers. Tell students that because no one helped some classmates achieve a higher score, everyone has to take the same lower score. This is what happens in a world of "same."

5. Go on to state that in the world of "same," everyone looks the same; dresses the same; eats the same food; has the same toys (cell phones); has the same hair, activities, personality, and sense of humor; makes the same amount of money; watches the same TV shows; listens to the same music; and has the same friends. Discuss with students why they would like or dislike this situation.

6. Ask students if they like being different. (They will say yes at this point.) Then ask them why they make fun of others and bully people because they are different.

7. Explain to students that if they like being different, they should tolerate differences in others. Show the steps of the skill of **"Tolerating Differences in Others"**:

   a. *Think about how you are similar to and different from the other person.*

   b. *Emphasize the shared interests/activities you have with the other person.*

   c. *Express appreciation and respect for the other person.*

8. Play the Beatles' song, "Let It Be," for the class. After listening to the song, tell the students, "Learn to be okay with you enough that you can let someone else have the freedom to be different from you!"

9. Introduce the "Let It Be" board (the butcher paper you have laminated). Explain to students that the board will be run like a Twitter. As part of their grade, each student will be required to "tweet" something once a week by writing a comment on how they can be appreciative of differences in other people. Have students use Twitter language and symbols, and have them use their Twitter ID name so you can track their messages each week without other students knowing who wrote a comment. (Or use whatever method will make it easier for you to monitor the board comments.) The board will serve as a constant visual reminder of how students think they can be appreciative of differences in other people.

10. Be sure to let students know that they will receive the actual grades they earned on their quizzes you returned earlier.

. . . .

When the students put all their things in one pile at the beginning of the activity, make sure they are separated enough so that their owners can easily find them later.

. . . .

YOLO. I appreciate my class!
@keepitreal88

Way to use your heads, table 4!
@xc-state013

So glad Gretchen knew about PH!
@sally2016

Lookin' good in our multicolored shirts back row!
@james2000

SECTION 4

Being the Difference

When students under-
stand their own value
and understand the value of
others, a platform is created from which students can
begin to respond to bullying and
take appropriate action based
on a more solid level of security
and confidence. This is where
students can find their voice and
change can start to occur.

Most students care about the feelings of
others and are anxious to help when a problem
arises. Giving them strategies to take action
brings satisfaction, accomplishment, and
control in their periodically out-of-control
and ever-changing world. They can begin to
see and believe that their actions CAN make a
difference that matters. They see hope.

Concepts Explored in Section 4:
- Responding to Bullying
- Strategies for Appropriately
  Taking a Stand
- Taking Action

Prezi through My Eyes

OBJECTIVES:

Social Skills: Students will learn safe ways to respond to bullying.

Executive Functions: Students will practice organization, task initiation, and curiosity while developing their Prezi by keeping track of their information, starting independently, and exploring new information.

MATERIALS NEEDED:

- Access to computers
- Paper
- Pencil
- Rubrics for evaluating and scoring Prezis
- Boys Town Social Skill "Responding to Bullying"

DIRECTIONS:

1. Create a teacher account on Prezi. Sign up for the free version at www.prezi.com.

2. As a class, view a Prezi, discuss its components, and have students begin creating their own Prezis.

3. Introduce the skill of **"Responding to Bullying"** and discuss each of its five steps.

   a. *Remain calm, but serious.*

   b. *Assertively ask the other person to stop the bullying behavior.*

   c. *If the behavior doesn't stop, ignore the person or remove yourself from the situation.*

   d. *If the behavior stops, thank the person for stopping. If appropriate and safe, explain how the behavior makes you feel.*

   e. *Report continued bullying or hazing to an adult.*

4. Give all students a copy of your login information so they can create their Prezis under your name. (Be sure to change your password once the activity is completed.) Or, if you prefer, have students create their own account.

5. Have students create a Prezi presentation individually or with a partner. They must have at least three different teasing, name-calling, or bullying scenarios in their presentation. They could also do a presentation scenario on disagreeing with someone appropriately or getting along

with people who don't click with them. Students can use historical accounts and information as long as they credit the source. They should include at least two positive ways and two negative ways they could respond to each of their three scenarios.

6. Give each student a sheet of rubrics (see the example at the end of the section) and have them use the rubric to score each Prezi presentation. If they see additional strategies in a presentation, ask students to write them in at the bottom of the rubric or on the back of the rubric sheet. Collect the rubric score sheets and keep them.

Having students vote on the most creative Prezi, the Prezi with the best advice, the most entertaining Prezi, and the Prezi that is most applicable or easy to use can also help motivate students. Small prizes like a "No Homework Pass" or having the title of King or Queen for the Day can be given to the winners.

FLIPPED CLASSROOM SUGGESTIONS:

Have students view several Prezis online. Ask them to list their favorite and describe what makes a Prezi interesting. Have them sign up for an account before coming to class.

Prezi on Responding to Bullying Rubric

		YES	NO
1.	Remained calm and brave/controlled their emotions	◯	◯
2.	Asked the other student or bully to stop/self-control	◯	◯
3.	Ignored the words or actions or removed themselves/self-control	◯	◯
4.	If it stopped, they thanked the other person/gratitude	◯	◯
5.	Reported continued bullying/social intelligence	◯	◯

6. *Other.* _____

_____

_____

_____

The Gong Show

OBJECTIVES:

Social Skills: Students will practice the skill of "Accepting Defeat or Loss" in a healthy environment for competition.

Executive Functions: Students will exhibit zest and humor while participating in the activities.

MATERIALS NEEDED:

- Video clip of *The Gong Show* ("Gene, Gene, The Dancing Machine," or "The Unknown Comic" are good clips; be sure to give proper credit when showing videos.)
- Some type of gong or buzzer

- Rubber mallets
- (Optional) Party blowers
- Possible bullying scenarios to act out (See sample list at the end of the section)
- Boys Town Social Skill "Accepting Defeat or Loss"

The Gong Show was an amateur talent show that was on TV from 1976 to 1980. Contestants would perform various acts for the judges. If the judges liked a contestant, he or she could continue to perform. If the judges did not like a contestant, they would take a mallet and hit a large gong. When contestants were "gonged," they had to stop and leave the stage. All the performers who were not gonged then competed for the grand prize of a few hundred dollars.

The worst act of the day got the "dirty tube sock." Interestingly, contestants displayed a good sense of humor, even if they knew they were going to get "gonged." (You also could use a different show like *America's Got Talent* and use a buzzer; however, using a vintage show such as *The Gong Show* can provide added humor and levity during this activity.)

DIRECTIONS:

Teacher could give an award for "Best Humor of the Day"!

1. Reference or play a video clip of *The Gong Show* so students have an idea of how it was played.

2. Divide the students into contestants and judges.

3. Point out how the real *Gong Show* contestants handled their defeat appropriately and review how the students should respond if they are "gonged" during the activity by introducing the skill of **"Accepting Defeat or Loss":**

   a. *Look at the judges.*

   b. *Remain calm and positive, and say "Okay" when the judges are pointing out something negative in the scenario.*

   c. *Reward yourself for trying* (maybe just patting yourself on the back).

4. Review the social skill of "Responding to Bullying" again, and instruct students to creatively incorporate the steps as they properly respond to teasing or bullying behaviors in their scenarios.

5. Have the student contestants act out some of the bullying or teasing scenarios. If the judges don't like the way students are presenting the scenarios, they can "gong" them or blow party blowers at them. The contestants can continue, but they have to change the way they are handling the scenario. This can continue for a while and can become funny as the students try to act out a scenario in an acceptable way.

6. If a judge "gongs" a contestant, that judge must be able to explain how the contestant was ineffectively handling the bullying behaviors or the bully.

7. Point out many positive and negative aspects of how the scenarios are presented.

. . . .

If using the party blowers, avoid this activity when you have a headache!

. . . .

FLIPPED CLASSROOM SUGGESTIONS:

Have students view several episodes of *The Gong Show* online, and ask them to come to class with their top two favorite shows.

Possible Bullying Scenarios

1. The "popular kids" won't let other students sit at their lunch table.

2. A few boys are standing in the hallway blocking access to a smaller boy's locker. The bigger boys look at him, but continue to joke around without moving, knowing he wants to get in his locker.

3. A girl walks into class and starts to put her books/things down on a table where two other girls are sitting. They quickly push their things over to an open table and tell the girl someone is already sitting there.

4. A larger girl is embarrassed to change into her PE clothes because some of the other girls tease her about being fat. They have called her names and one of the girls has even taken a picture of her on a her cell phone and threatened to send it to other students.

5. Jesse is a middle school boy who likes to sing and dance. The other boys have started calling him names and have posted rumors about him on Facebook.

6. Mandy and Taylor are friends. They live in the local trailer park and ride the bus home every day. Three other girls ride the same bus, but they get off at the housing division before the trailer park. The three girls have started calling Taylor names like "slut" and "trailer trash."

7. One day in class, three boys decide to sit at a table Zeek usually sits at. Zeek, who is much bigger than the other boys, doesn't like it and tells the boys to move. They tell him "No" and he responds by saying, "I'm not having a good day, so you better move or you'll be sorry!"

The Cyberbully

OBJECTIVES:

Social Skills: Students will practice displaying appropriate control.

Executive Functions: Students will demonstrate self-control by refraining from reacting publicly to negative comments.

MATERIALS NEEDED:

- Access to computers
- Class blog already set up and running
- Paper

- Pencil
- Cyberbullying question sheet
- Boys Town Social Skill "Displaying Appropriate Self-Control"

The Internet has become an integral part of our lives. It has improved communication speed and provides us a wealth of information right at our fingertips. As much as it has helped us, though, it does have its drawbacks. One of those is that it has made it much easier for people to say negative things online that they probably wouldn't say to someone's face. The Internet has facilitated bullying and allows comments or videos to be circulated to many in just a matter of seconds, potentially creating a cruel disadvantage for our young people today.

DIRECTIONS:

1. Post a negative comment about one class to your other classes on the class blog/website. (Just make sure it is not offensive or inappropriate.) Post an assignment there as well, so that all students have to go there to see it.

2. Instruct students to write their reaction to the post within five minutes of reading it, but do not have them post their response. Instead, have students bring it to class the next day.

3. Introduce the skill of **"Displaying Appropriate Self-Control"**:

   a. *Monitor your feelings and your verbal and nonverbal behavior.*

   b. *Use relaxation strategies to manage stress.*

   c. *Speak calmly, clearly, and specifically.* (In this activity, write down a response instead of speaking it.)

   d. *Accurately represent your feelings with well-chosen words.*

   e. *Use language that will not offend others.*

4. The next day, gather the students' initial responses and save them for comparison.

5. Have students use Facebook, Instagram, MySpace, other social media sites, and various search engines on the Internet to gather data on cyberbullying.

6. After the students have compiled their data, have each student construct and post an informed response to the earlier negative comment you posted on the class blog/website.

7. Compare and contrast the two sets of responses.

. . . .

 Springboard students' research with the following questions (see worksheet):

   a. What is cyberbullying?

   b. Does it happen in real life, and if so, how often does it occur?

   c. Why is it harmful?

   d. Is it legal?

   e. Is there anything you can do about it?

. . . .

FLIPPED CLASSROOM SUGGESTIONS:

Have students view a video on cyberbullying or find their own sources, and answer the questions under "Tips." They should bring their answers to class and post their initial and researched responses to the negative comment you posted on the class blog/website.

ADDITIONAL RESOURCES:

Video on cyberbullying

Cyberbullying

Write down answers to the questions below.

1. What is cyberbullying? _____
   _____
   _____
   _____

2. Does it happen in real life, and if so, how often does it occur?_____
   _____
   _____
   _____

3. Why is it harmful?_____
   _____
   _____
   _____

4. Is it legal?_____
   _____
   _____
   _____

5. Is there anything you can do about it?_____
   _____
   _____
   _____

Stuck... or Stick Together

OBJECTIVES:

Social Skills: Youth will explore the ways and advantages of resisting negative peer pressure.

Executive Functions: Students will use this activity to further develop their social intelligence.

MATERIALS NEEDED:

- A paper outline of a person, cut out ahead of time (it's best to use construction paper because it will be difficult to remove sticky items from it)
- A piece of bubble gum for each student
- Medium to large old phone book
- Boys Town Social Skill "Resisting Peer Pressure"

DIRECTIONS:

1. Give each student a piece of gum to chew.

2. Talk about what bullying is and how it affects people.

3. Ask students to bully the paper cut-out "person" by going up to it, one at a time, and saying something mean or derogatory to it. At the same time, have them smash their wad of gum onto the paper person. Then have the students write their name next to their wad of gum. (Remember to advise students to use appropriate language.)

4. After every student has done this, lay the paper person down on the floor and point out that the bullying words stuck to the person.

5. Next, ask each student to completely remove their gum from the paper person without tearing the paper. (This should be difficult to do.)

6. Ask the following questions:

   a. How does this relate to bullying someone?

   b. Can we ever completely take back the things we say or do to a person? Why or why not?

c. What is the best way to not have the gum stick to the paper person? (By not putting it there in the first place.)

d. Why do some of you give in to bullies even if you are not the victim?

e. What can you do?

7. Teach the skill of **"Resisting Peer Pressure."**

a. *Look at the person.*

b. *Use a calm, assertive voice tone.*

c. *State clearly that you do not want to engage in the inappropriate activity.*

d. *Suggest an alternate activity. Give a reason.*

e. *If the person persists, continue to say "No."*

f. *If the peer will not accept your "No" answer, ask him or her to leave, or remove yourself from the situation.*

Students can be "stuck" by bullies and try to be brave and take care of things on their own (which usually just makes them continue to feel "stuck"), OR they can stick together with others and stand up to the bully.

To illustrate:

8. Show students an old phone book and tear out one of the pages. Ask a volunteer to come forward and tear that page in half. Point out how easy it was and ask the students how that compares to a bully or someone who is mean picking on just one person and getting everyone else to do it too.

9. Ask for another volunteer to come up and try to tear the whole phone book in half. You might have several students try this. Even if someone could tear it in half, point out how much more difficult it is. Ask how this could relate to bullying.

You are more of a target if you are alone. If you have a group to stand with you or stand up for you, it will be much more difficult for someone to bully you (just like not being able to tear the whole phone book in half).

10. Possible questions:

    a.   What if you don't have a group?

    b.   What if you do have a group and you see someone else being picked on?

    c.   Does supporting or helping someone mean that you have to hang out with them after school? Could you end up liking the person as a friend?

    d.   Are you being open-minded or closed-minded when you say you don't like someone before you ever get to know them?

    e.   How can you help find solutions during conflicts with others?

    f.   How can you choose good friends? (Review the Boys Town visual on choosing friends with students.) What advantages are there to having good friends? Do bullies make good friends?

    g.   Finally, do you believe that you can make a difference or that a small group of students can make a difference against bullying? Why or why not?

    h.   Would you rather be "Stuck" or "Stick Together"?

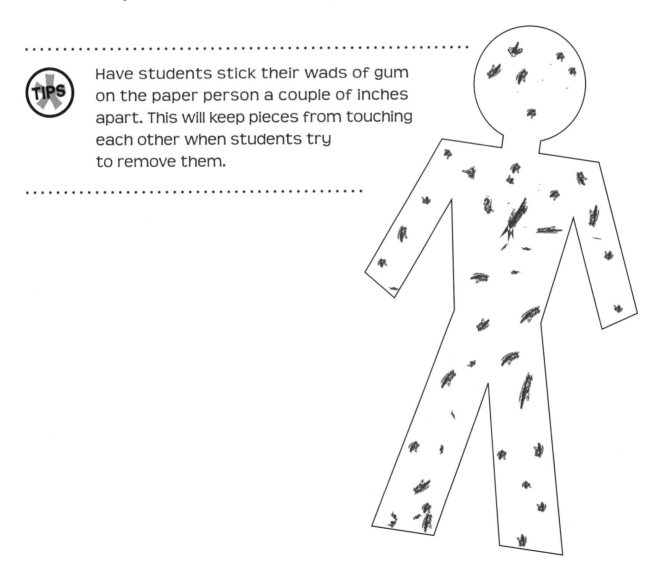

TIPS

Have students stick their wads of gum on the paper person a couple of inches apart. This will keep pieces from touching each other when students try to remove them.

Texting or Se"X"ting

> **OBJECTIVES:**
>
> **Social Skills:** Students will learn the steps to the skills of "Resisting Negative Peer Pressure" and "Reporting Others' Behavior."
>
> **Executive Functions:** Students will strategize self-monitoring/self-control skills and the meaning of prudence or discretion when encountering peer pressure.

MATERIALS NEEDED:

- Free version of the QR reader app downloaded on phones or iPads (see instructions below under "Additional Resources")
- iPads and/or cell phones
- Paper

- Pencil
- QR Video Questions worksheet (on CD)
- Boys Town Social Skill "Resisting Negative Peer Pressure"
- Boys Town Social Skill "Reporting Others' Behavior"

. . . .

 Students may have knowledge of what se"X"ting is, but they may not realize that se"X"ting, sexual harassment, or sexual bullying is more than just sending sexually suggestive or explicit photos, and can include things like crude, sexually oriented jokes, sexual comments, and unwanted touching or groping.

. . . .

DIRECTIONS:

1. Set the groundwork for identifying what se"X"ting is and determining what students already know about sexual harassment and bullying. If this was brought up in someone's Prezi presentation in an earlier activity, you could review it again.

2. Put three to five QR codes for videos around the room. You may use more or fewer of these or ask students to watch three out of the five videos.

3. Download a free version of the QR reader on a mobile device. If you don't have enough mobile devices for all students, have them work in groups.

4. Have students capture the QR code on their device, watch the video at their desk or a designated spot, and answer the questions you provide. (See the "QR Video Questions" worksheet at the end of this section.)

5. Review the students' answers to these questions as a class. On question #3, you will probably get several reasons for why teens participate in se"X"ting. Some will say that they want to feel accepted, or they are naive. They also might say they are trying to please another person. But eventually lead them back to the topic of peer pressure.

6. Ask the students to define peer pressure and give examples of it. Then ask the students how they could respond to peer pressure. After they have given their ideas, introduce the skill of **"Resisting Negative Peer Pressure."**

    a. *Look at the person.*

    b. *Use a calm, assertive voice tone.*

    c. *Clearly state that you do not want to participate.*

    d. *Suggest an alternative activity and give a reason.*

    e. *Continue to say "No" if the person persists.*

    f. *If the person will not accept "No," remove yourself from the situation.*

7. Have the students convert these strategies into a list for resisting peer pressure through a text, email, or Facebook. Ask how that list of strategies is different from how a person would respond when he or she is face-to-face with another person. If a person is not directly in front of us, does resisting peer pressure change? Discuss how it changes. Students also need to know that they may lose a boyfriend or friend by standing up to peer pressure. Talk through these scenarios and ask the students to generate a list of ways they could handle these types of outcomes.

8. Ask the students to define "prudence" and "discretion." (Prudence means being careful about one's choices; discretion means not taking unnecessary risks.)

9. Contrast these terms with the practice of se"X"ting. Ask the students to collaborate and come up with a list of self-monitoring strategies to help them use discretion in their choices.

    a. Recognize what is going on inside their body/mind.

    b. Recognize what is going on in their environment.

    c. Recognize how se"X"ting could negatively affect their relationships.

    d. Set some appropriate boundaries.

- Imagine a series of circles radiating out from your body.
- Picture the people you know in one of those circles, depending on the level of closeness you share with them.
- Disclose personal information only to those who are in the closest circles.
- Touch others only in ways that are appropriate for your boundaries and send only appropriate photos.
- Respect the boundaries of others.

10. Encourage students to report any inappropriate talk, touch, or electronic messaging of any kind by using the steps to **"Reporting Others' Behavior":**

    a. *Stay calm and tell the other person to stop his or her behavior.*

    b. *Remove yourself from the situation.*

    c. *Find an adult and get his or her attention appropriately.*

    d. *Honestly report what has happened.*

    e. *Answer all questions honestly.*

    f. *Thank the adult for listening.*

You can post the QR codes to a blog or hand a student a printed QR code if he or she has been absent. Because of the seriousness of this content, you may want to spend more than one class period on this topic.

ADDITIONAL RESOURCES:

After you have downloaded the QR reader app to your mobile device, you can start to make QR codes. Find a video or website you want the students to view. With your computer cursor, copy the website URL address. Then go to the QR reader and find the "Creator" tab; under this tab, you should see a "+" symbol. Click on the "+" symbol and a dropdown should appear with choices of what you can create. To copy a website, you will want to choose "WebURL." You can then paste in the website URL address and click on "Create." The website/video will now be under your "Creator" tab. You can then share or print off the QR code.

QR Video Questions

1. Is se"X"ting a big deal or not? _____
    _____
    _____
    _____

2. Define se"X"ting in your own words. _____
    _____
    _____

3. Why do you think young people your age would take part in se"X"ting? _____
    _____
    _____
    _____

4. Can se"X"ting be dangerous or it is pretty harmless?_____
    _____
    _____
    _____

5. Can se"X"ting ruin your reputation? If you said yes, would this be permanent?_____
    _____
    _____
    _____
    _____

Go Bananas
for Class Meetings

OBJECTIVES:

Social Skills: Students will learn the appropriate way to report another youth's behavior to an adult.

Executive Functions: Students will practice developing their zest by actively participating in the class meeting and activity, and enhance their citizenship by working well as a member of a group during the team-building activity.

Exclusion and intimidation can be very difficult to observe among youth. There are times when it is blatantly obvious, but most of the time it is not. Youth may appear outwardly friendly toward other youth, and say all the "right" things in front of an adult, but they can be extremely crafty at giving one of their peers the silent treatment. Exclusion also takes the form of simply pretending that someone doesn't even exist (e.g., knowingly turning your back on someone when he or she approaches).

Most of the time, exclusion is premeditated, intentional, and relational aggression. However, there are times when students are just genuinely oblivious to the world around them and unintentionally exclude someone. Some bullies will use intimidation to get what they want from other students, such as getting to sit where they want. Again, most of the time, the supervising adult does not even know this has taken place.

MATERIALS NEEDED:

- White board or chart paper
- Different scenarios of peer issues (in case nothing is brought up during the class meeting)
- Tape, staplers, string, glue, paper clips, masking tape
- Banana (1 per group)
- Large paper plates (1 per group)
- Plastic knives
- Boys Town Social Skill "Reporting Others' Behavior"

DIRECTIONS:

1. Have students sit in a circle so they are facing each other. Open the meeting by reminding them that this is a time when they can feel free to share whatever they want about the class. Remind them to not interrupt when others are talking and to not use names when giving examples.

2. Let the students share their thoughts, and when problems are brought up, have the class brainstorm ways they could be solved or handled better. Write these on a piece of chart paper or on the white board as a visual reminder. If the students don't bring up anything, then share a scenario to get the conversations rolling.

3. After you have concluded that part of the meeting, it is important to let students know that if there is still an issue they want to report, there is an appropriate way to do that. Post the following guidelines for the skill of **"Reporting Others' Behavior"**:

Make sure the bananas are somewhat ripe for best results.

   a. *Look at the teacher or adult.*

   b. *Use a calm voice and ask to talk privately.*
     (A student may have to wait if the adult is busy.)

   c. *Describe another person's behavior.*

   d. *Tell why you are making the report*
     (note the difference between reporting and tattling).

   e. *Answer any questions the adult might have.*

   f. *Thank the adult for listening.*

NOTE When students advocate for themselves, it boosts their self-esteem and confidence.

4. Finish the class meeting with this team-building activity or another one of your choice.

   a. Place half of a fairly ripe or yellow banana on a large paper plate at each table of four students. Ask the students to peel the banana and cut it into as many parts as they want (use plastic knives).

   b. When all groups have finished cutting their banana, place Scotch tape, staplers, string, glue, masking tape, and paper clips on the tables. Tell the students they now have 5-10 minutes to put the banana back the way it was before they peeled and cut it. This includes putting it back in its peel.

   c. After students have tried to "fix" their bananas using the things you have given them, display all of the bananas for everyone to see and laugh at.

   d. Ask the students how this relates to gossiping and bullying. Help them realize that the answer is that once they say hurtful, hateful words to or about someone else, they can never get those words back or make things the way that they were. We can never "fix" people so they are exactly as they were before the hurtful words were spoken. Therefore, we should think before we speak.

Putting It All Together

These final lessons are group activities that students can organize and initiate themselves. They are designed to help educate the uninformed and to prompt others into joining the quest to reduce or eliminate bullying that occurs daily in our schools. They are designed to celebrate diversity among individuals while helping students analyze and identify the strengths they have that can contribute to the progress of our society. The lessons challenge individuals to MAKE a Difference in the "Life of One."

Concepts Explored in Section 5:
- Working with Others
- Analyzing Skills to Combat Bullying
- Valuing Diversity
- Identifying Strengths to Contribute to Community Progress
- Using Community Resources

Putting It Into Practice

> **OBJECTIVES:**
>
> **Social Skills:** Students will learn strategies for working with others on larger projects.
>
> **Executive Functions:** Students will identify and utilize planning and task-initiation behaviors when planning an anti-bullying campaign.

MATERIALS NEEDED:

- Jenga blocks
- Access to computers
- Paper
- Pencil
- Boys Town Social Skill "Working with Others"

DIRECTIONS:

1. Build a large Jenga block tower before class begins.

2. To begin the activity, tell the students that the tower represents a victim of bullying.

3. Call on several volunteers to come up to the tower and give an example of a type of bullying they have learned about. After they state their example, have them pull a Jenga block from the tower. Continue this until someone makes the tower fall.

NOTE The Jenga block tower is somewhat like our students. When students are together and respectful of each other, they are solid and there aren't any holes (or hurts). But when someone starts saying or doing mean things, or excluding a student, or spreading rumors, a little bit of that student gets chiseled away, just like taking a block away. Sometimes, taking one or two blocks out isn't a very big deal. But if more blocks are removed, the tower won't look as sturdy even though it may remain standing. And when too many blocks are taken out, the tower crumbles, just like a person can. An individual can get so beat down that it takes a very long time to get back to normal. Sometimes, those students can never completely rebuild their own towers.

. . . .

4. Ask students to take out a piece of paper and answer several questions. Make the first few questions about anything that's been covered in the bullying unit. (The answers students give are not the important part of this activity.) The last question should be:

> *"What is the difference between KNOWING ABOUT bullying and what to do about it and KNOWING ABOUT bullying and ACTUALLY DOING something about it?"*

The campaign should be student-led and action-based.

5. Introduce the idea of an anti-bullying campaign. Ask the students to start planning and implementing a campaign that will create more awareness in your school about all aspects of bullying. Tell them to be creative! This campaign can look any way students want it to look for their school! Before beginning, go over the steps to **"Working with Others"** with students:

    a. *Identify the tasks to be completed.*

    b. *Assign tasks to each person.*

    c. *Calmly discuss all ideas.*

    d. *Work on tasks until they are completed.*

The "E" Mighty and the "I" Mighty

OBJECTIVES:

Social Skills: Students will reflect on what might be motivating bullies to behave a certain way, and task analyze skills they think the bully would benefit from learning.

Executive Functions: Students will practice generating and sequencing complex actions.

MATERIALS NEEDED:

- 2 paper cut-outs of a bully figure (butcher paper works well). Label one "Entitled" and the other "Insecure/Inferior."
- Markers
- Paper
- Pencils
- "Bullying T-Chart" worksheet
- Your choice of Boys Town Social Skill(s) as examples

DIRECTIONS:

1. Introduce two types of bullies.

   a. **The "E" Mighty, or the "Entitled" Mighty.** These bullies feel they are entitled to whatever they want. Therefore, they treat people however they want because they believe they should get to make the rules depending on how they feel; it is their "right" to do so.

      Describe a scene from the movie, "Willy Wonka & the Chocolate Factory," where Veruca Salt is in the egg room, yelling, "I want it NOW!"

   b. **The "I" Mighty, or the "Insecure/Inferior" Mighty.** These bullies feel socially, financially, or ability inferior to their peers, so they try to elevate themselves while holding others down. This is how they gain their sense of security. Because of their lack of confidence and social intelligence, they intimidate and humiliate others so they appear stronger.

2. Have students write down the type of bully they usually come into contact with and the category that bully falls under. Have them discuss how this could be difficult because they may not know the bully well.

3. Ask students to brainstorm the names of some skills they think the bully should learn.

4. Introduce the concept of "**Task Analysis**":

   a. *Keep the skill specific and focused, and label the skill.*

   b. *List three to five behaviorally specific steps that need to be performed in order to use the skill.*

   c. *Put the steps in the appropriate order.* (You can use one of the Boys Town Social Skills as an example so that students understand what you want them to do.)

5. As a class, have the students select a handful of the skill labels they identified and task analyze each one into a set of three to five behavioral steps.

6. Have students write those skills on the cut-outs of each type of bully.

7. Leave the cut-outs hanging in the classroom as a visual reminder.

· ·

Our society has become very child-centered, with many adult schedules revolving around children's schedules. Everything is done for the comfort of the child. Adults rescue them at every turn and try to make their lives perfect and wrinkle-free. Children grow up thinking that they "deserve" whatever they want without really having to sacrifice anything like hard work, time, or energy to get it. This activity is designed to help children think about their roles and responsibilities in social development.

· ·

ADDITIONAL RESOURCES:

A possible reference for "Willy Wonka & the Chocolate Factory," a 1971 movie directed by Mel Stuart that was based on the book, "Charlie and the Chocolate Factory," by Roald Dahl.

NAME:_____

Bullying T-Chart

Write down the similarities and differences of these types of bullies.

The "E" Mighty *Entitled*	The "I" Mighty *Insecure/Inferior*

Let Your Voice Be Heard

OBJECTIVES:

Social Skills: By writing about and analyzing anti-bullying strategies, students will learn the importance of using community resources in getting their message out to the public.

Executive Functions: Students will display social intelligence by recognizing how to take a stand against bullying.

MATERIALS NEEDED:

- Several newspapers
- Phone book
- Access to Internet
- Paper
- Pencil
- Boys Town Social Skill "Using Community Resources"

DIRECTIONS:

1. Have students write a statement, paragraph, short story, or poem about bullying or how to decrease its occurrences among peers in their school. These should be insights students have gained from everyday bullying occurrences they've seen, strategies for addressing bullying they've learned, or firsthand experiences of being bullied.

2. Ask students to brainstorm ways they could get their messages or thoughts out to the public. One example would be to contact the local newspaper.

3. Have students view editorials and comments from other individuals in various newspapers so they have a good feel for how to make their message fit the format.

4. Have students revise their writings, checking spelling and grammar. Make sure the writings are in publishable form.

5. Have students go over the steps to **"Using Community Resources"** to determine how to contact and utilize the local newspaper as a community resource:

Have a Plan B in case the local newspaper will not print the writings.

   a. *Identify your exact needs* (wanting to publish their thoughts in the newspaper).

   b. *Use phone books or an Internet search service to locate phone numbers for individuals at the local newspaper who can assist them.*

   c. *Look in the newspaper for contact information or ideas for additional help.*

6. Make a copy of the students' writings to display throughout the school or at an event such as Parent/Teacher Conferences.

Contact the local newspaper before beginning this activity to see if there is a possibility it will publish the students' ideas and writings.

FLIPPED CLASSROOM SUGGESTIONS:

On the class blog or website, post links to "How to write articles for a newspaper." Have the students listen to or view several posts, and come to class with a list of five tips for writing a good paragraph, statement, poem, or short story for a newspaper.

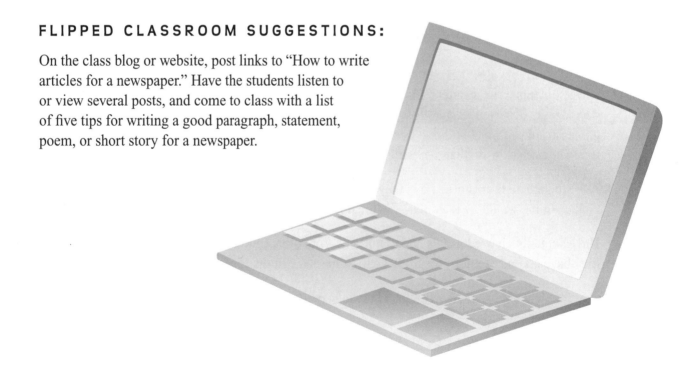

Progress Party

OBJECTIVES:

Social Skills: Students will accurately identify their own strengths and how they can be used to contribute to progress in our communities.

Executive Functions: Students will recognize that their efforts and unique abilities can contribute to and improve the future of our communities.

MATERIALS NEEDED:

- Paper
- Scissors
- Glue

- Materials to make and decorate hats
- Boys Town Social Skill "Accepting Self"

 People wear different hats within our communities. They use their gifts and talents to contribute to the progress of our communities and nation. It is important for youth to recognize that they, too, have a unique responsibility and privilege of contributing to that same progress, through the utilization of their own unique talents and abilities.

DIRECTIONS:

1. Ask students to make a hat that represents their uniqueness in terms of abilities, talents, and personality and how their uniqueness helps or could help their school, community, and nation to progress. Provide supplies for them to make their hats (paper, craft supplies, patterns of hats, cardboard tubes, etc.).

2. After students have had time to construct a hat that they feel represents them, ask them to write down why their hat looks the way it does. Tell them the importance of the skill of **"Accepting Self"**:

Teachers can make one, too.

   a. *Accurately identify your own strengths.*

   b. *Express pride in your strengths or accomplishments.*

   c. *Accentuate your strengths to compensate for your weaknesses.*

   d. *Use self-accepting phrases when talking about your tastes, style, etc.*

3. Have all students share with the class why they designed their hat the way they did. Please note that this might be difficult for some students. They may not feel confident or may not have been told by others that they have value. Be sure to affirm students as you go, and emphasize that each of them has his or her own unique value and abilities that will contribute to improving our communities now as well as in the future.

For progress as a **school, a community,** and a **nation, we must think and act differently.**

4. After all students have shared about their hats, write the following statement on the board:

    "For progress as a school, a community, and a nation, we must think and act differently."
    Discuss the meaning of this again.

5. Time to celebrate. Since the students already have their hats, it would be a good time for a class party that celebrates uniqueness and diversity. Providing treats, music, etc., would be a bonus for the students.

. . . .

 Be careful to affirm each student's strengths even if you do not particularly agree that what a student has identified as a strength really is one for him or her. Students need to know they can contribute.

. . . .

White Out Day

OBJECTIVES:

Social Skills: Students will assess their own bullying behavior in terms of the progress they have made and then participate in a class celebration in honor of their anti-bullying efforts.

Executive Functions: Students will display zest in actively participating in the anti-bullying activities.

MATERIALS NEEDED:

- Strips of paper
- Pencils or markers
- "White Out Day" questions
- Small (approx. 8") squares or strips of white fabric (you will need one for each student)
- Fabric markers or paint

DIRECTIONS:

1. Ask students to participate in a "White Out Day," where they all wear white to school.

2. Give each student a strip or square of white fabric. Have students use the fabric markers or paint to write an anti-bullying word or message on their piece of fabric. Allow for drying time. (This works best if these are made the day before the "White Out Day.") Remind the students that historically, individuals would wave a white flag in times of conquest to indicate their intentions to surrender or to signal a time of truce or peace.

3. Ask students to reflect on their own behavior. Assessing one's own behavior can be challenging and requires the ability to view oneself with an honest, critical eye. To help students make an accurate assessment of their behavior, ask them to follow these steps:

   a. Make a list of your strengths and weaknesses when it comes to taking a stand against bullying.

   b. List situations where you have successfully used anti-bullying measures.

   c. Assess your future potential in carrying out some of the anti-bullying suggestions the class has discussed during activities.

4. Give each student three strips of paper. Ask them to write their answers to each of the following questions on the strips of paper (one answer per strip of paper):

    a. Through your own efforts, how have you taken a stand against bullying?

    b. Through group efforts, how have you reduced bullying in our school?

    c. What do you still need to work on?

5. Plan an activity that celebrates the group's efforts to reduce incidences of bullying. Plan an anti-bullying rally or convocation. On a smaller scale, have an administrator or other teachers make anti-bullying statements on the intercom periodically throughout the day. Whenever the students hear an anti-bullying remark, they can wave their white cloths! Remind the students to enthusiastically participate and cooperate in the group activity and to use a pleasant voice when talking with others in the group.

Allow for paint or fabric marker drying time. Plan the group activity many days in advance so it can resemble a celebration.

White Out Day

Each student gets three strips of paper. Please write your answers to each of the following questions on the strips of paper (one answer per strip of paper).

Through your own efforts, how have you taken a stand against bullying?

Through group efforts, how have you reduced bullying in our school?

What do you still need to work on?

APPENDIX

Skills and Their Steps

SECTION 1: *THE UNMASKING*

Greeting Others

1. Look at the person.
2. Use a pleasant voice.
3. Say, "Hi" or "Hello."

Introducing Yourself

1. Look at the person. Smile.
2. Use a pleasant voice.
3. Offer a greeting. Say, "Hi, my name is...."
4. Shake the person's hand.
5. When you leave, say, "It was nice to meet you."

Making New Friends

1. Look at the potential new friend.

2. Use a pleasant voice and introduce yourself.

3. Share some of your interests and hobbies.

4. Listen to the other person's name and areas of interest.

5. Plan appropriate activities, with permission.

Choosing Appropriate Friends

1. Think of the qualities and interests you would look for in a friend.

2. Look at the strengths and weaknesses of potential friends.

3. Match the characteristics of potential friends with activities and interests you would share.

4. Avoid peers who are involved with bullying, drugs, gangs, or breaking the law.

SECTION 2: *RECOGNIZING THE LABELS*

Tolerating Differences in Others

1. Examine the similarities between you and another person.

2. Take note of the differences.

3. Emphasize the shared interests, tastes, and activities between you and the other person.

4. Express appreciation and respect for the other person as an individual.

Making an Apology

1. Look at the person.

2. Use a serious, sincere voice tone, but don't pout.

3. Begin by saying "I wanted to apologize for..." or "I'm sorry for...."

4. Do not make excuses or try to rationalize your behavior.

5. Sincerely say that you will try not to repeat the same behavior in the future.

6. Offer to compensate or pay restitution.

7. Thank the other person for listening.

Accepting an Apology

1. Look at the person who is apologizing.

2. Listen to what he or she is saying.

3. Remain calm. Refrain from making sarcastic statements.

4. Thank the person for the apology; say, "Thanks for saying 'I'm sorry'" or "That's okay."

Communicating Honestly

1. Look at the person.

2. Use a clear voice. Avoid stammering or hesitating.

3. Respond to questions factually and completely.

4. Do not leave out details or important facts.

5. Truthfully take responsibility for any inappropriate behaviors you displayed.

SECTION 3: *VALUING OTHERS*

Disagreeing Appropriately

1. Look at the person.

2. Use a pleasant voice.

3. Say, "I understand how you feel."

4. Tell why you feel differently.

5. Give a reason.

6. Listen to the other person.

Expressing Empathy and Understanding for Others

1. Listen closely as the other person expresses his or her feelings.

2. Express empathy by saying, "I understand...."

3. Demonstrate concern through your words and actions.

4. Reflect back the other person's words by saying, "It seems like you're saying...."

5. Offer any help or assistance you can.

Tolerating Differences in Others

1. Examine the similarities between you and another person.

2. Take note of the differences.

3. Emphasize the shared interests, tastes, and activities between you and the other person.

4. Express appreciation and respect for the other person as an individual.

SECTION 4: *BEING THE DIFFERENCE*

Responding to Bullying

1. Remain calm, but serious.

2. Assertively ask the person to stop the bullying behavior.

3. If the behavior doesn't stop, ignore the other person or remove yourself.

4. If the behavior stops, thank the other person for stopping and explain how the behavior makes you feel.

5. Report continued bullying or hazing to an adult.

Accepting Defeat or Loss

1. Look at the person or members of the team who won.

2. Remain calm and positive.

3. Say "Good game" or "Congratulations."

4. Reward yourself for trying your hardest.

Displaying Appropriate Self-Control

1. Monitor your feelings and your verbal and nonverbal behavior.

2. Use relaxation strategies to manage stress.

3. Speak calmly, clearly, and specifically.

4. Accurately represent your feelings with well-chosen words.

5. Use language that will not offend others.

Resisting Negative Peer Pressure

1. Look at the person.

2. Use a calm, assertive voice tone.

3. State clearly that you do not want to engage in the inappropriate activity.

4. Suggest an alternative activity. Give a reason.

5. If the person persists, continue to say "No."

6. If the peer will not accept your "No" answer, ask him or her to leave, or remove yourself from the situation.

Reporting Others' Behavior

1. Find the appropriate adult or authority figure.

2. Look at the person.

3. Use a clear, concerned voice tone.

4. Specifically state the inappropriate behavior you are reporting.

5. Give a reason for the report that shows concern for your peer.

6. Truthfully answer any questions that are asked of you.

SECTION 5: *PUTTING IT ALL TOGETHER*

Working with Others

1. Identify the tasks to be completed.

2. Assign tasks to each person.

3. Discuss ideas in a calm, quiet voice and let everyone share their ideas.

4. Work on tasks until they are completed.

Task Analysis

1. Keep the focus of the skill limited.

2. Identify behaviors of the skill as steps.

3. Use specfic and observable terms.

4. Put the steps in order of performance.

Using Community Resources

1. Identify your exact needs.

2. Use phone books or an Internet search service to locate contact information for resources.

3. Contact the resource and ask for help.

Accepting Self

1. Accurately identify your own strengths and weaknesses.

2. Express appropriate pride in your accomplishments.

3. Compensate for weaknesses by accentuating your strengths.

4. Use self-accepting phrases when talking about your tastes, style, etc.

BIBLIOGRAPHY

Eiseley, L.C. (1978). *The star thrower.* Harcourt Brace Jovanovich.

Fox, S. & Stallworth, L.E. (2010). The battered apple: An application of stressor-emotion-control/support theory to teachers' experience of violence and bullying. *Human Relations, 63,* 927-954.

http://edu.glogster.com

https://en.wikipedia.org/wiki/Masquerade_ball

http://www.historyofmasks.net/

http://www.prezi.com

http://www.safetyweb.com

http://www.toondoo.com

Stuart, Mel (1971). *Willy Wonka & the Chocolate Factory* [Motion Picture]. United States: Warner Brothers.